By the same author:
Ulster & Its Future After the Troubles (1977)
Ulster & The German Solution (1978)
Ulster & The British Connection (1979)
Ulster & The Lords of the North (1980)
Ulster & The Middle Ages (1982)
Ulster & St Patrick (1984)
The Twilight Pagans (1990)
Enemy of England (1991)
The Great Siege (2002)
Ulster in the Age of Saint Comgall of Bangor (2004)
Ulster Blood (2005)
King William's Victory (2006)
Ulster Stock (2007)
Famine in the Land of Ulster (2008)
Pre-Christian Ulster (2009)
The Glens of Antrim (2010)
Ulster Women – A Short History (2010)
The Invasion of Ulster (2010)
Ulster in the Viking Age (2011)
Ulster in the Eighteenth Century (2011)
Ulster in the History of Ireland (2012)
Rathlin Island (2013)
Saint Patrick's Missionary Journeys in Ireland (2015)
The Story of Carrickfergus (2015)
Ireland's Holy Places (2016)
The Conqueror of the North (2017)
The Story of Holywell Hospital: A Country Asylum (2018)
Patrick: A Saint for All Seasons (2019)

THE PICTS: THE PAINTED PEOPLE

Dedication
To the memory of Mrs Muriel Harbinson.

THE PICTS: THE PAINTED PEOPLE

BC – Fifth Century AD

Michael Sheane

ARTHUR H. STOCKWELL LTD
Torrs Park, Ilfracombe, Devon, EX34 8BA
Established 1898
www.ahstockwell.co.uk

British Library Cataloguing-in-Publication Data.
A catalogue record for this book is available
from the British Library.

ISBN 978-0-7223-4978-6
Printed in Great Britain by
Arthur H. Stockwell Ltd
Torrs Park   Ilfracombe
Devon EX34 8BA

Picts is a name given to the inhabitants of the Scottish Highlands during the first millennium AD. They first appear in history when the Roman Empire was invading Britain. In mythology, the Picts appear as a mysterious race whose history was unknown, and they became a people apart. They have left behind a number of carved stones, many of which are still visible on the landscape. Many of these stones bear esoteric designs, from the Isle of Skye to Aberdeen and from Shetland to Fife. These carvings have remained uninterpreted, despite many attempts to understand them.

The lifespan of the historical Picts lasts from AD 300 to 850. A list of kings has survived in mediaeval manuscripts, giving their reign lengths. This list starts at the beginning of the fourth century AD and ends in the ninth. Among the reliable sources of testimony is Bede's *Ecclesiastical History of the English People*, a book completed in AD 731. The lives of the early Scottish saints also provide information about the Picts. But a glance at the Irish annals gives the Picts as a race apart.

The Picts are enigmatic, for we are not sure when they disappeared from history. Archaeological data also provides a lot of information about these ancient people, who painted themselves before they went into battle against the Roman legions and before other conflicts.

Before the arrival of the Picts, their territory was perhaps inhabited by an earlier race. Conquest of Caledonia by the Romans was considered by the emperors Augustus and Caligula, but postponed until the middle of the first century. Agricola, the Roman governor of Britain, sailed around the coast of Scotland and carried on campaigns in the Highlands. The natives of the Highlands are described by the Roman historian Tacitus as having reddish hair and large limbs, a proud people. The Romans braved the cold and rainy weather of the Highlands and Lowlands.

In AD 83 Agricola marched across the River Forth at the head of an invading force of 25,000 men. The Picts retaliated immediately. The great clash of arms occurred in late August or early September at Mons Graupius – a name that later inspired the naming of the Grampian Mountains. Tacitus names one of the Pictish leaders as Calgacus, meaning 'the swordsman'. As many as 30,000 warriors would have assembled to face the Roman legions, but the Pictish chariots were soon overcome by the Roman cavalry. Mons Graupius was a resounding victory for the Roman Empire over the Picts. This could have brought Agricola's final conquest of Britain in sight, but the result did not turn out to be as decisive as he might have wished. Two-thirds of the barbarian horde survived the onslaught and managed to return to their homes.

Now the summer campaigning season was waning, and there was no time to establish control over an area as vast as the Scottish Highlands. Agricola was sure, however, that he could not consolidate his victory, especially with autumn coming and with large numbers of Picts still lurking in the hills. The task of running them out presented an appalling prospect. The Roman army duly turned about and returned to winter quarters in the south, leaving a number of forts to guard the glens of Perthshire; hostages were taken, but the Roman advantage was lost.

Agricola nominally held sway over all the territory south of the Moray Firth, but the political situation deprived him of an opportunity to consolidate his gains. The Emperor Domitian, jealous of Agricola, upon hearing of the victory, ordered him to leave Britain and return to Rome. The historian Tactitus tried to portray the victory at Mons Graupius as a great success, but he could not hide the fact that the Picts remained unconquered. Calgacus and his warriors were still at large. One small consolation for the empire was that the Roman fleet, completing its operations along the eastern seaboard and sailing around the top of Scotland, saw the Picts, giving them a final display of Roman power before sailing down the west coast.

Lots of information was gathered about the geography of Scotland and its Picts and other tribes, and the information was put down on a map. The map is unique, and a fascinating document which shows how the British Isles appeared to Roman eyes. It identifies the other tribes of the Highlands and indicates the approximate positions of their territories. The map shows sixteen tribes inhabiting Scotland. A number of Roman forts are also marked. The map places the Caledonii tribe across the central Highlands; much of what is now Aberdeenshire is shown as lying within the territory of the Taezali; while Fife appears to be the home of the Venicones tribe.

Within a decade of Agricola's withdrawal from Scotland, the Romans were pessimistic about ever conquering the Highlands; the forts established in Perthshire during the campaign of AD 80–84 were abandoned. A new legionary fortress at Inchtuthil, on the north bank of the River Tay, was dismantled before its construction was completed; wooden watchtowers were erected, but these were abandoned by AD 90. In the Scottish Lowlands the garrisons lingered on for ten years; but as the second century dawned in the empire, there was a need for more manpower on the Danube, causing a major withdrawal of troops from Britain. The northern frontier fell back again, shrinking the limits of the empire to the Tyne–Solway isthmus.

In the early years of the second century, northern barbarians launched an attack upon Roman Britain. It is not known if the Picts were among these people, but the invasion left a trail of devastation in its wake. The situation was serious, for the Emperor Hadrian ordered the building of a wall along the Tyne–Solway frontier. The great work was started in 122 or 123 and was still in progress when Hadrian's successor, Antoninus Pius, launched a campaign in the North. The new emperor's task was not only to subdue the Highlands, but to maintain peace in the Scottish Lowlands.

The Emperor now entrusted the campaign to one Quintus Lollius Urbicus, who launched his attack on Scotland in 140. Within a few years, Roman power was restored along the Tay Estuary, and new forts were built to make the gains permanent. The imperial frontier was fixed slightly to the south, being marked by a barrier – the Antonine Wall – only consisting of turf. Sixteen forts were erected in its forty-mile length, accommodating 600 men. Also, several of Agricola's forts were maintained as forward outposts.

The turf wall was perhaps built in response to Antoninus's thirst for power, rather than as a purely defensive project. For a while it became the northern border of the empire and made Hadrian's Wall redundant. But it did not survive long as a frontier, and it was briefly abandoned in the 150s, for revolts were taking place in the Pennines, before being permanently abandoned in the following decade. The final withdrawal came after the death of Antoninus in 161, which allowed his successors to downsize the northern frontier army. A handful of forts beyond the Forth were still garrisoned, but the imperial boundary shrank back to Hadrian's Wall.

Before the close of the second century, the Caledonians were assailing the Scottish Lowlands with increasing ferocity. The Romans recorded the overrunning of Hadrian's Wall between 180 and 184; the attack was brief, but it was a major defeat for the empire and a great achievement for the barbarians. The great stone wall was recovered, but all the forts to the north of it were for the meanwhile temporarily abandoned to the enemy.

At the opening of the third century, the situation was uncertain. The Romans now faced hostility between the Firths of Clyde and Forth; one opponent was their old enemy the Caledonians, who carried on an uneasy treaty with Rome. The other hostile tribe was the Maeatae, whose lands corresponded to present-day Stirlingshire. According to the annals, this tribe occupied territory north of the Antonine Wall, and to the north of this again were the other barbarians.

Ptolemy's second-century map shows the Caledonii tribe covering a wide area of northern Scotland, from west coast to east. It is clear that all of these tribes formed some kind of loose political entity under some kind of high kingship. Ptolemy shows twelve tribes in the area, perhaps amalgamated in his lifetime. This was an heroic age and an Iron Age society. Unity was forced on these peoples rather than enforced confederation.

By 197, the Emperor, Septimius Severus, emerged victorious from a serious civil war in Gaul, or France, and he had to deal with the growing menace on his borders. On the northern frontier in Britain, Maeatae were still belligerent and were being held back only by large gifts of Roman cash, while the Caledonians were on the verge of breaking a fragile treaty with Rome. During the early years of the third century Roman diplomacy maintained control of the frontier, but in 205–6 two barbarian confederacies launched an invasion. Britain's governor appealed to Rome for more troops, or for the direct involvement of the Emperor himself.

Emperor Severus wanted to give his sons some experience in diplomacy and warfare away from the decadence of Rome. Now Severus arrived in Britain with a large army in 208. He took personal command of the political situation, marching north, crossing the Forth–Clyde isthmus to attack the Maeatae. There was fierce fighting and the barbarians carried on a guerilla war on their home territory until Rome beat them into submission. The Emperor now wanted to establish a massive legionary force to confront the barbarians in Perthshire, at Carpow, on the Tay.

In 210 the Maeatae rose again, but at a time when

Severus was stricken with illness; the task of crushing the uprising was given to Caracalla, who applied brutal solutions, giving the barbarians an opportunity to fight against Rome. Now Severus died and was succeeded in the purple by Caracalla, who now consolidated the Antonine frontier, but he soon realised that it was impractical to contain the North. He at length made peace with the barbarians, withdrawing his forces from the Forth–Clyde line while he himself hurried to Rome.

The construction of the new fort at Carpow had already begun, but was now abandoned. It was now impossible for the empire to maintain itself in Britain. No Roman general would ever again march towards the Tay to threaten the tribes who lived in the hills and glens. From that moment onwards, the destiny of the far north lay in the hands of the barbarians.

In the final years of the Roman occupation of Britain, the Picts made their appearance out of the previous mythology; they arrive suddenly in the historical records, but what of their origins? Historians talk in terms of the problem of the Picts. What was their language, culture and social structure? Their origins may start in the final years of Roman rule in the island of Britain, after the end of the Severan military campaigns. The third century appears to have been a period of relative peace in Roman Britain, even in Scotland.

At Colchester, sometime in the 220s or 230s, a man called Lossio Veda was commemorated on a tombstone. He was a barbarian that supported the Roman regime in Britain. He may have spoken Latin and was therefore literate, but he retained devotion to the pagan gods. He worshipped Mars Medocius, a Romanized Celtic deity who may have been a god of the North. The memorial description describes Lossio as a nephew or grandson of a man called Vepogenus, but little is known about this family. It is hard to compute why this family settled so far south of their homelands.

At this time there may have been an easing of relations

between the empire and Caledonia. More information comes from Dio Cassius, who refers to a conversation between the Empress Julia Domna, wife of Severus, and the wife of the Caledonian chieftain Argentocoxos, at a time when the two women were chatting while their husbands negotiated a peace treaty on the northern frontier. The Romans were critical of the loose morals of the barbarians, and in response the barbarian women criticized the loose morals of Roman ladies. This conservation may have been invented so that Dio Cassius was able to pass judgement on Julia Domna's promiscuity by contrasting her behaviour with that of the Picts; free love was perhaps practised by these barbarians of the Scottish Highlands. Lossio's memorial description and Dio Cassius's piece of gossip about third-century morality provide useful information, but they do not prove that the Romans and the Picts along with the other tribes were living happily side by side. The situation in the Highlands seemed to be less tense in the 220s. Hadrian's Wall appeared to be a secure boundary between Scotland and the North and the imperial province of Britannia.

North of Hadrian's Wall, the Romans kept a close watch over the native tribes. Although these forts marked the northern limit of Rome's power, the Romans took the opportunity of gathering information about the Picts; the most westerly of these outpost forts lay at Netherby, just north of Carlisle, and was known as the Fort of the Scouts. Military intelligence was gathered by various covert means, such as spying, but also by means of open-air assemblies of the native tribes; these meetings took place at regular intervals and at chosen sites, usually in the presence of Roman officers, to whom the Picts and the other tribes were answerable. At each assembly the tribes aired their grievances and settled their own disputes, so the Romans were able to spot troublemakers. Each assembly, or *locus*, served a particular region lying north of Hadrian's Wall, where *loci* had long since been abandoned. To facilitate the process the *loci* were sited at ancient landmarks where the tribes usually settled for either public or military ceremonies in pre-Roman times.

Thus the regional meetings of the inhabitants of north-western Scotland were held at 'the place of the god Mabon Locus Maponi', which was almost certainly the great boulder known as Clochmabenstane on the northern shore of the Solway Firth. Further north, around the shores of the Firth of Forth, the assembly at 'the place of the Manau district' gathered at a similar sacred rock (Locus Manavi). The ancient name of this landmark still survives in the town and county name Clackmannan; today the ancient boulder sits on top of a pillar in the town's main square, although its original location was at Lookaboutye, a few hundred metres away.

Britons of the Tweed and Clyde Valleys also met with Roman officials at chosen *loci*, but the positions of these sites is unknown, as is the whereabouts of what may have been a more northerly assembly near the Firth of Tay. The modern historians' incomplete knowledge of sites is matched by ignorance of how often the assemblies were held and how matters were conducted. It is likely that the system of scouting operations and regional meetings was accepted by Romans and Picts alike throughout the third century AD. It permitted the Britons living beyond Hadrian's Wall to govern their own affairs under imperial protection, and at the same time the Roman Empire could maintain control as far north as the Tay.

On an economic level, the system freed the imperial treasury from the huge financial burden of maintaining a permanent presence in Stirlingshire and southern Perthshire, and in the forts lying along the Antonine Wall. However, the frontier zone also remained relatively stable until the last years of the century, when an old enemy with a new name came upon the scene from the Highlands in the person of the Picti. In 297, the document known as the 'Panegyric of Constantius Caesar' mentioned two tribes of barbarian folk as troublesome to the empire in Britain. One of these was the Hiberni; the other group was the Picts. The identity and ancestry of this new 'nation' was made clear some years later when another Latin text referred to the woods and marches of the Caledonians and other Picts. Also later, in the 360s, the soldier historian Ammianus Marcellinus stated that the Picts were divided into two peoples – the Dicalydones and Verturiones; the latter appear on Ptolemy's second-century map, but the former were Caledonii under a variant of a former name. The confederacy of tribes of Agricola's time had now split into two subdivisions.

Ammianus cites a number of raids upon Roman Britain in 364, and he identifies the Picts as the culprits alongside Saxons, Scots and a very savage race called the Attacotti. The Saxons were still based in northern Germany at this time, and had not yet made the permanent bases in Britain that would at length turn them into Anglo-Saxons. The designation 'Scots' was used by Ammianus and his peers as a broad label to distinguish any speakers of Scots Gaelic from those that spoke other Celtic languages, such as the Britons and Gauls. The term did not, however, denote the inhabitants of 'Scotland', for no such entity existed in Roman times.

The Scots of the fourth century were various Gaelic-speaking groups on either side of the Irish Sea – namely, the people of Ireland and Argyll. The Attacotti were a mysterious people whose origins and identity are unknown, but they may have come from Ireland or the Hebrides and were regarded as being distinct from the Picts and the Scots. Neither Ammianus nor his fellow historians could explain the origins of the name Picti. The belief that the Caledonians and the Verturiones were the main components of this 'confederacy' suggests that both Dunkeld and the later Picti province lay within its territory; the Verturiones were core elements of the Picti nation.

The heartland of the Picts extended from Perthshire to the Moray Firth, but the full extent of the lands of the Picts was much greater. As we have seen, the Caledonians of the second and third centuries were a confederacy of tribes. By the end of the third century these confederacies had acquired a new name for themselves, of which the Latin name Picti was a Roman variant. Overall power within the nation had fallen into the hands of two main subgroups – the Caledonians and the Verturiones. The relationship of these tribes to the Pictish 'nation' as a whole, and to each other, can only be guessed at. Each tribe was clearly a distinct entity, but altogether they were regarded as Picts. Caledonians may have been the most important group. There is no mention of the fourth-century Maeatae, whose warriors had posed such a threat to Roman Britain on the Forth–Clyde isthmus.

Were the Maeatae excluded from the Pictish nation? Were they a separate group whose cultural affinities hold them apart from the Picts? They may have been recognised as non-Picts, but no sources reveal the precise origin of the Picts, and it is this enigmatic group that we shall examine next.

The word Picti is a Latin term meaning 'the painted people'. Its Roman name origin suggests that it was a nickname given by troops on the imperial frontier to barbarians lurking in the wild lands beyond the Roman walls. The main characteristic of the Picts was that they tattooed their bodies, and this practice distinguished them from the other tribes. The likely origin of their Roman name is that it was a term of military slang – a term of derision. Picts appear to have had a name of their own, but it is not known what it was. Neither they nor their neighbours have recorded a name for posterity in any of the surviving sources. Among the Britons, who in the fourth century were under the power of Rome, the Picts were called the Priteni; this term survived the evolution of the Brittonic language into Old Welsh, and in the form of 'Prydyn' it came not only to denote the Picts, but their homeland as well. 'Priteni' and its variant 'Pritani' were not originally labels applied exclusively to the Picts, but also to their homeland. Both are very ancient terms that the earliest Greek and Roman travellers used when referring to all the peoples of Britain, and both words may have meant 'the people of the designs'. Later the Romans of Julius Caesar's time encountered the word Pritani, but altered it to 'Britanni' and restricted its application to those tribes that were to eventually come under the rule of the empire.

'Britanni' was in turn adopted by the natives that had been conquered by the Romans, and in the form of 'Brittones' (Britons) became the name they used for themselves. The other word, Priteni, soon lost its original meaning, but as the age of the empire progressed the Britons of the imperial province began to use the name for the hostile barbarians who lived in the Highlands, beyond the Forth–Clyde isthmus. Later, Britons and Romans alike started to call these barbarians Picti. Since the Picts were part of a Celtic culture and linguistic milieu, the Picts may have called themselves by a name similar to the ancient term of Priteni; it is also thought that they may have used a term that has been lost to history. Perhaps this word when heard by Roman ears sounded like the Latin slang term Picti and was adopted not only by the Roman troops on the northern frontier, but also in the annals of the Roman Empire. The Picts' own name for themselves perhaps carried the same meaning as both Picti and Priteni, and signified 'the people of the designs' or 'the painted people'.

To Roman eyes these designs were the most striking aspect of the Picts. Had the tattooing not seemed unusual, the frontier garrisons would have coined another word other than Picts from the repertoire of barrack-room slang. The habit of adorning the skin with painting is what distinguished the Picts from the other native groups in the British Isles, and also gave them a unique and visible identity. To the Roman scout, gazing across the river at a group of tribesmen on the opposite bank, any warrior with painting was a Pict rather than a Briton or a Scot. But what would this Roman scout have seen? Claudian the poet, who recited at the imperial court, spanned the years around AD 400 and gave an answer to this question when he wrote about a number of Picts, making reference to body painting. But Claudian was not the only Roman writer to cite this phenomenon, which had been seen long before the time of Julius Caesar. In the first century BC, when the legions first came into contact with the Picts, the custom of painting bodies was already common across many parts of Ireland. Caesar wrote that body painting in woad – a dark-blue dye – made them seem formidable in battle, but he makes no mention of specific tribes and does not say if woad was tattooed after being applied to the skin.

In the early third century AD, the Greek writer Herodian observed that the barbarians of northern Britain painted their bodies with a range of designs, which included the representation of animals. Four centuries later, the Christian monk Isidore of Seville believed that the practice of using needles to imprint designs had earned the Picts their name. If this historian is correct, it may support the view that the Picts made the decoration permanent with the use of blue dye; this practice had been clearly abandoned by their neighbours, the Britons, whose ancient customs had been eroded by two centuries of Roman rule.

In later times in the empire tattooing was regarded by non-Picts as being barbaric and primitive – the taint of an uncivilized people. The modern image of the painted Pict has been regarded in the same way, and has added weight to the view that the Picts were less sophisticated than their neighbours.

Let us turn to matters of geography. There is little precision involved in Roman perceptions of which lands were inhabited by Picts and which were inhabited by Britons. To complicate matters, the fourth-century writers perhaps used the term Picti as a vague label for all barbarians inhabiting the Forth–Clyde isthmus, not merely those who dwelt in the Pictish lands. Nor was the term restricted to mainland Britons. The imperial poet Claudian used it when writing of the Picts living in 'Thule', which was usually identified as the Shetland Isles. But the poems were works of eulogy rather than of history or geography and were not written to provide an accurate gazetteer of peoples and places. There may, however, be some historical basis to the idea of a greater Pictland stretching from the Hebrides to the North Sea, and from the Forth–Clyde isthmus to Orkney and Shetland. For a more precise indicator of where the Picts lived, a useful clue is the distribution of names of places called 'Pit', which derives from a word meaning a portion of land in the ancient Pictish language. Names beginning with 'Pit' are found all over the Highlands, but have an eastern distribution between the Firths of Tay and Moray.

The region also embraces the ancient Caledonian heartland and it is where the writers of the early historic period placed many of the main events in Pictish history. It can therefore be identified as a centre of Pictish culture in the sense of it being where most identifiable traits of that culture originated or became concentrated. Outside of this heartland, in areas as far afield as Orkney and Skye, local populations consider themselves to be no less Pictish than the people of Perthshire or Aberdeenshire or Moray, where the distinctive 'Pit' place names are most numerous.

As will be seen over the following pages, the most

recognizable elements of Pictish culture are visible over wide areas of northern Scotland, and are not confined to those regions where 'Pit' is a common prefix in place names. The imprecise geography of the Roman writers is often frustrating, but perhaps they were right to assign the name Pict to any band of barbarians who emerged from the Highlands and Islands. From Fife to the Isle of Skye, and from Shetland to Tay, the native inhabitants were almost certainly part of the Pictish 'nation' of tribes or clans.

What, then, were the key cultural traits that allowed this area to be called Pictland? First of all, a common language was known throughout the Highlands. This knowledge is not gleaned from ancient documents written in the Pictish tongue – no such texts have survived, if they ever existed. Evidence of Pictish language comes from the names of places and peoples, as far as these can be identified from contemporary sources, preserved in the landscape of modern Scotland. The earliest records of Pictish place names come from Roman writers, of which the geographer Ptolemy is the richest source of information. It has been already noted that Ptolemy's map of the known world (second century) includes the British Isles, showing not only the names of tribes, but also various places that were significant to Rome. These names were no Latin inventions, but in many cases were simple Latinizations of native originals.

Ptolemy's map cites forty population groups in Scotland and names settlements associated with them, along with some topographical features. The latter ranged from large islands, such as Skye (Secris) and Mull (Malaius). A look at Ptolemy's map confirms that the majority of these names are of Celtic origin. They were given verbally by natives to Roman observers, who wrote them down for translation into Latin. The map confirms that all the people of Scotland during the Roman Empire used a Celtic language when giving a name to their lands and to their communities. The characteristics of this language show that it was part of a group known to linguists as P-Celtic. This group includes Gaulish and Brittonic – the languages of Gaul and Britain – but it excludes the Goidelic or Q-Celtic languages, of which the Gaelic of Ireland, Scotland and the Isle of Man are modern representatives. Brittonic is the ancestor of Welsh, Cornish and Breton and was the language spoken by most of the peoples of Britain under the empire. Linguists believe that Pictish was akin to Brittonic, basing this conclusion not only on the language of the Highlands of Ptolemy's map, but also by comparing modern place names in Scotland and Wales. The prefix 'Aber', for example, which means river mouth, is found a lot in the Highlands in names such as Aberdeen and Abernethy. The Welsh word *perth*, meaning a bush or copse, is borne by the Scottish city of that name, and it is also found in less obvious contexts, such as Muir of Pert.

The prefixing 'Pit', referred to above, was originally a Pictish word and is related to Welsh and Cornish *peth* (a thing), and to Breton *pez* (a piece). In Gaul, or France, where the natives spoke P-Celtic, related to Brittonic, the equivalent word was something like *petia*. Some 300 place names north of the Firth of Forth begin with 'Pit', denoting a portion of land. There is, as already stated, a marked concentration of 'Pit' names in the east of Scotland, from Fife through Perthshire to Aberdeenshire.

The occurrence of the prefix in a handful of names along the Great Glen and on the western mainland opposite Skye shows that these areas were places where the Picts held pieces of land. However, many of the suffixes attached to 'Pit' were not given by P-Celtic speakers. Later Gaelic replaced Pictish as the language of the Highlands in the ninth and tenth centuries.

But the 'Pit' names are so numerous that these names with their unique P-Celtic prefix are regarded as important evidence of the Brittonic character of the Pictish language. There are equivalent names in Wales, Cornwall and Brittany, suggesting that units of land were apportioned in a different way in these areas. This implies that the Picts and Britons did not deal with ownership of land in the same manner, or it may point to a different application of landholding. This sets the Pictish language apart from the main branch of Brittonic, spoken by people living south of the River Forth.

Over a long period of time the two languages diverged for a number of reasons. A key factor was the Roman influence in the frontier region, where a strong military presence may have disrupted native communications to turn northern Stirlingshire and southern Perthshire into a linguistic borderland; this and other factors may have hastened the separation of Pictish Brittonic from mainstream Brittonic, with each branch evolving separately. The result was a linguistic boundary running along a cultural and political frontier along the Forth Valley. Historians have been puzzled by a number of names on Ptolemy's map which appear to incorporate words of non-Celtic origin.

As recently as half a century ago there was a revival

of interest in Pictish history and culture and language in northern Scotland during the Roman period and the early historic period, where there was a survival of native ways. From this comes the suggestion that elements were not only non-Celtic, but also non-Indo-European, and suggests great contributions associated with Pictish society. The notion of a non-Indo-European origin for the Picts arose in the late nineteenth century and held much appeal for those who liked to imagine that the prehistoric people of Scotland are as puzzling as the Basques or Etruscans. This theory lasted for some time and was still being promoted in the 1930s and 1940s. It retained a foothold even after publication, in 1955, of Kenneth Jackson's paper on the Pictish language, which appeared in a book entitled *The Problem of the Picts*. Jackson was one of the many pre-eminent Celtic historians of his time, and his papers remained the definitive work on Pictish linguistic matters for the next four decades. His main conclusion was that the Picts spoke not one language, but two, these being a P-Celtic dialect closely related to Brittonic alongside a non-European tongue. The former, he suggested, had given way to the latter during the first millennium BC, when the native language of the British Isles became obsolete after the migration of the Celts from continental Europe. Jackson surmised that in Pictland a native pre-Celtic culture had survived for ritual purposes and was preserved throughout the Roman imperial period and beyond, until the Gaelic culture extinguished both it and the Pictish P-Celtic tongue in the ninth century AD. Jackson demolished any notion that the Picts should be regarded as non-Celtic or non-Indo-European, and placed them among the Celtic nations of

Britain. But recent scholarship has discredited his theory of two Pictish languages after identifying many of the presumed non-Indo-European names as being P-Celtic after all.

Whilst a number of pre-Celtic words have been retained in place names and personal names, it is now clear that the Picts spoke only one language; this was a Celtic tongue, a close relation of the Brittonic dialect spoken by their neighbours south of the Forth and Tay. The Picts had their own theory about their origins, but no first-hand account has survived; what has survived is a story of Pictish beginnings, contained in a curious origin-legend promoted by their neighbours. This was committed to writing at a time when the Picts had already become absorbed by the mediaeval kingdom of Scotland, and is not therefore a Pictish text. It states that the first king of the Picts was Cruithne, whose seven sons divided Pictland between them.

The name Cruithne is simply a Gaelic equivalent of the Brittonic name Priteni, a name, as we have seen, given to them by Romanized Britons living south of the walls. The presence of a Gaelic name raises suspicions about the legend's true origins, for the Picts were not Gaels and would have been unlikely to give a foreign name to an ancestral figure. This suggests that the name and the story were created by non-Pictish folk in a Gaelic-speaking environment in Scotland or Ireland.

In the origin-legend, the mythical Cruithne reigned for 100 years, his sons reigning for a further quarter of a millennium; and they ruled over a number of districts. Legends such as these are not, of course, a source of true history, but were devised for particular purposes to promote specific interests. In the case of the Pictish origin-legend, the names of the seven sons of Cruithne are derived from territorial divisions, which appear to relate in some way to later earldoms and mediaeval kingdoms in Scotland. Fib is the ancient name for Fife, while Fotlaig is an ancient name for Atholl. Circinn is a name associated by mediaeval sources with Angus and the Mearns, while Fortrenn is the genitive form, in Gaelic, of the area around Moray, commonly called Fortriu. As seen previously, Fortriu was associated with the Latin tribal term Verturiones, both names referring to the same people and to their territory. Cait is obviously Caithness, but Ce and Fidach are less certainly identifiable. One possible clue is that the Aberdeenshire hill Bennachie might have preserved the same name, as has previously been seen. If this is at all certain, the province of Ce could be equated with the mediaeval earldoms of Mar and Buchan.

A twelfth-century account of the Cruithne story clarifies the geography of the seven divisions, linking Ce explicitly to Mar and Buchan, while placing Fidach in the east at Ross. It is interesting that only the eastern and central Highlands are encompassed by the legend, leaving Argyll and the Isles excluded from this vision of Pictish origins. The exclusions suggest that the creators of the legend, whether they were not themselves Picts or Gaels, regarded the Gaelic west as a non-Pictish zone.

The legend of Cruithne is best understood as political propaganda originating after the end of the Pictish period to promote a particular ideology at a time of crisis and instability; looking beneath the story, it can be seen that its creators sought to preserve the mediaeval earldoms of eastern Scotland and link them to a common ancestor.

Some historians wonder if equating the seven provinces or sub-kingdoms of the Picts with regions of mediaeval Scotland might be incorrect, for the sources may be uncertain, so the equations are unlikely to be geographically precise. But even allowing for the late and probably non-Pictish origin or the tales, earlier and more reliable sources show that they contain an element of truth. The Gaelic annals in Ireland provide contemporary information for the era of the Picts, and refer to three of the seven provinces – namely, Fortriu, Circinn and Atholl. These three areas were already named during the Pictish period, but perhaps the other four had a similar history; the sources did not allow this matter to be pursued much further.

The actual extent of a particular province of the Picts is unlikely to be uncovered. It may never be known if the boundaries of Cait were the same as those of the earldom of Caithness. A problem is the location of Fortriu. If it corresponds to Sthearn and Menteith, as was formerly believed, are modern historians right in placing it much further north?

The story of Cruithne is not the only Pictish origin-legend.

A rather different story was recorded by the historian Bede in his *Ecclesiastical History of the English People*. Bede was a monk at Jarrow in Northumbria who lived in an age when there was a lot of communication between the Picts and their English neighbours across the Firth of Forth. He was writing in the early eighth century, and he records that the Picts had sailed from their homelands in Scythia, a wild region notorious for its winds in eastern Europe, beyond the reach of classical civilization. After being blown about by these winds, the Picts in a few warships eventually landed in Ireland. Their request to remain as settlers was refused by the Gaels, who claimed that their country had no room for two nations. The Gaels asked the Picts to settle across the sea in Britain, and offered to help them, presumably in a military capacity, if the native population showed any resistance.

In a final act of friendship, the Gaels gave women to the Picts, who appeared to have no power of their own; the gift was bestowed on condition that, whenever the succession to a Pictish kingdom remained in doubt, the new king should be chosen from the female royal line. Bede added that this custom was still used by the Picts of their own time – a custom known as matrilineal succession. Bede's synopsis of the story has a distinctly Irish orientation and presumably originated in Ireland. Later versions of the tale show Gaelic influence by including the mysterious ancestor Cruithne. All versions, including Bede's, perhaps derive from a legend that was well known in Ireland before the eighth century. This legend was merely an attempt by the Irish Gaels to explain why the Picts differed in certain aspects of their culture from other natives of northern Britain; the Gaelic-speaking Scots of Argyll, and the Britons that lived south of the Forth–Clyde isthmus were embraced in this system. Neither this tale nor the story of Cruithne answers the fundamental questions: who were the Picts and what did it mean to be Pictish? At this juncture, these queries could be turned on their head by asking if the Picts really were as different from their neighbours as Bede and other writers suggest. To answer these questions, we must look inside Pictish society to see how it worked. In the meantime, the focus switches to observe the impact made by the Picts during the final phases of the Roman Empire in Britain. This means again, and for the last time, that we must rely upon the work of the Roman historians.

Let us look at the end of Roman Britain. In 367, according to Ammianus Marcellinus, the many barbarian nations, whose war bands had been plundering for many years, combined their efforts to launch a huge attack on the Roman province of Britain – a well-planned assault. Such cooperation between barbarian tribes was completely unexpected in the provinces or colonies of the Roman Empire. Spies were at work along the northern frontiers of the empire. They were no doubt associated with the spies or secret agents who had scouted beyond Hadrian's Wall in the previous century. In 367 they cooperated with the barbarians by providing key geographical and military information in return for a share in the loot. These attacks overwhelmed the imperial forces; they thrust them into disarray.

Some high-ranking officers were killed during the conflicts. Roman Britain now lay at the mercy of the barbarians, and York was overwhelmed and became the barbarian headquarters. The defenceless inhabitants, who had relied upon Roman protection for 300 years, were brutally plundered and terrorized. The Roman emperor sent relief forces to Britain to restore order, but it was two years before peace was restored in the province, to re-establish the Pax Romana.

But the situation did not remain stable for long; by the close of the fourth century, Britain again was under attack by the barbarians. The Picts were attacking Rome on the northern frontiers of the empire in Britain. By the end of the first decade of the fifth century, the military situation in Britain had become perilous. The troops were withdrawn to help the situation in Europe as the barbarians encroached upon the empire. The leading citizens of the empire took matters into their own hands, and they formed their own armies to defend themselves against the Picts. Finally, in the year 410, they were told by the Emperor Honorius that there would be no more assistance; this dismissive response effectively ended Roman power in Britain. The Picts jumped for joy when they heard the news and seized the opportunity to raid their southern neighbours without fear of meeting with the Roman legions. This was a picture drawn by other historians when the legions now retreated from Britain. Most of these accounts appear to be accurate.

South of Hadrian's Wall, the Roman bureaucracy had disintegrated. From its ruins there arose a number of petty kingdoms. Gildas, a monk recording the withdrawals, was scornful of the situation. His greatest scorn was reserved for Maglocunus, a sixth-century monarch in northern Wales, who epitomized everything that was corrupt and degenerate about Britain's post-Roman leadership. Gildas believed that the conditions that helped the men to seize power meant they had to solve their own political problems without imperial help.

More attacks followed from the north and west, the

Picts leading the way. In Gildas' eyes, the Picts and the Scots were quite barbaric.

The fifth century was a time of great trouble for the Picts and their neighbours; the result was that the northern garrison was no more after 400 years of peace. By 400 there may have been only a small Roman presence along the line of Hadrian's Wall – a far cry from the garrison that had patrolled the area. After 410 there was no more pay due from the imperial coffers, so the disillusioned soldiers vanished into local communities, upon which they fell to the same level.

The old network of forts fell as the Picts attacked. A few forts were reused as strongholds by the new Pictish leaders who appeared at this time. Gildas referred to a brief remanning of Hadrian's Wall by the Britons. It appeared that there would now be nothing to keep the Picts at bay; the great wall between Tyne and Solway was now deserted.

However, the new powers that had arisen from the collapse of the Roman province quarrelled among themselves. Gildas mentions the recruitment of Saxon mercenaries to defend the lowland Britons from attacks by the Scots and Picts, but these troops were confined to eastern areas and were settled no further north than Yorkshire. Gildas' account of affairs on what is now the Anglo-Scottish border threw up some ugly scenes of bearded, half-naked Picts using hooked spears to drag helpless Britons from the parapet of the wall, but this report has no basis in fact. It painted a terrifying image of savage barbarians for the secular and religious elites of the southern part of Britain, to whom Gildas addressed his words.

The real situation in the North during the fifth century was in fact quite different. Far from lying open to Pictish attack, the lands of the Tyne and Solway were protected by a buffer zone extending northwards as far as the Forth and Clyde. In earlier times, this region was ruled directly from Rome, while the Antonine Wall remained firm. Later, when the frontier had fallen back to Hadrian's Wall, the people that lay between the two walls maintained close links with the empire and were regarded as subjects or allies of Rome.

The main tribes of this area were the Novantae of Galloway in the south-west, the Selgovae in the centre, the Votadini in the east and the Damnonii in the north-west. These tribes were among those who had formerly assembled under Roman supervision and were designated *loci* and whose lands had been ruled by exploratores from the outpost forts. The territories of the Votadini and Damnonii bordered on the Highlands and therefore faced the Picts, whom they resisted in the final phase of imperial rule.

After the withdrawal in 410, a resurgence of independence among the Britons increased the defensive role of these tribes to make them a powerful bulwark against Pictish attack. Sometimes they were defeated or plundered, but by the end of the fifth century they still held the Forth–Clyde line intact. By then the tribes had evolved into kingdoms. The Votadini, whose kings had ruled from Edinburgh, emerged in the sixth century as the realm of Gidoddin. To the west the Damnonii created a kingdom at the citadel of Dumbarton. They regarded themselves as being distinct from the Picts.

By 500 the southern Britons were emerging from the

upheavals of the post-Roman period with kings and kingdoms of their own. For the Picts, the departure of Rome did not leave their neighbours helpless and open for ravaging. On the contrary the chaos of the early fifth century swept away the last remnants of the ailing imperial garrison. Thus, by playing a major role in the collapse of Roman rule, the Picts had paved the way for powerful new rivals to enter the political arena.

SELECT BIBLIOGRAPHY

A. Ritchie, *Picts* (Edinburgh, 1989).

D. J. Breeze, *Roman Scotland* (London, 1996).

F. T. Wainwright (editor), *The Problem of the Picts* (Edinburgh, 1995).

I. Henderson, *The Picts* (London, 1967).

M. Carver, *Surviving in Symbols: A Visit to the Pictish Nation* (Edinburgh, 1999).

T. Clarkson, *The Picts: A History* (Edinburgh, 2008).

W. A. Cummins, *The Age of the Picts* (Sutton, 1995).